To Grandma Kaiser who gave me the idea for this book. We miss you very much! And to Bill and Kathy Outlaw who shared their house in Leakey, Texas with us. We love you and appreciate all you've done.

Buford was born a city bear,

Buford the Bear
Written and Illustrated by
Lori Kaiser

Another great book in the Xavier Series!

Published by
Carpe Diem Publishers
17401 Betty Blvd.
Canyon, TX 79015
806-433-6321

www.carpediempublishers.com

© Copyright, 2011 by Carpe Diem Publishers. All Rights Reserved. No portion of this book may be reproduced, stored in a retrieval system, or transmitted, in any form or by any means, electronic , mechanical, photocopying, recording, or otherwise without prior written permission from publisher.
Printed in the United States of America
ISBN 978-0-9845761-7-3

Often he'd dream of a country scene:

When he got to the country
he couldn't believe
All the sounds and the smells
and the pretty green trees.

www.ingramcontent.com/pod-product-compliance
Lightning Source LLC
Chambersburg PA
CBHW042045290426
44109CB00001B/34